To _____

Love _____

FRIENDS ARE SPECIAL

A TRIBUTE TO THOSE WHO ACCEPT, SUPPORT, & CARE

COMPILED BY
LUCY MEAD

GRAMERCY BOOKS
NEW YORK

This 2001 edition is published by Gramercy Books ™, an imprint of Random House Value Publishing, Inc. 280 Park Avenue, New York, N.Y. 10017.

Gramercy Books™ and design are trademarks of Random House Value Publishing, Inc.

Random House
New York • Toronto • London • Sydney • Auckland
http://www.randomhouse.com/

Printed and bound in Singapore

Interior Design: Karen Ocker Design, New York

Library of Congress Cataloging–in–Publication Data

Friends are special / compiled by Lucy Mead.
    p. cm.
  ISBN 0-517-16312-8 (hardcover)
  1. Friendship--Quotations, maxims, etc. 2. Friendship--Poetry. I. Mead, Lucy.

PN6084.F8 F494 2001
177'.62--dc21

00-037664

Friends are Special

Friendship is certainly the finest balm
for the pangs of disappointed love.

JANE AUSTEN

Say what you mean to do…and take it for granted you mean
to do right. Never do a wrong thing to make a friend or keep
one…you will wrong him and wrong yourself by equivocation
of any kind.

ROBERT E. LEE, *Memoirs of Robert E. Lee*

Friendship is constant in all other things,
Save in the office and affairs of love.

WILLIAM SHAKESPEARE

Animals are such agreeable friends, they ask no questions,
they pass no criticisms.

GEORGE ELIOT

If we would build on a sure foundation in friendship, we must love friends for their sake rather than for our own.

CHARLOTTE BRONTE

A friend in power is a friend lost.

HENRY ADAMS, *The Education of Henry Adams*

A friend married is a friend lost.

HENRIK IBSEN

We cherish our friends not for their ability to amuse us, but for ours to amuse them.

EVELYN WAUGH

A friendship founded on business is better than a business founded on friendship.

JOHN D. ROCKEFELLER

Friendship is the inexpressible comfort of feeling safe with a person, having neither to weigh thoughts nor measure words.

GEORGE ELIOT

I can always get along with an honest man.

HARRY S. TRUMAN

Only solitary men know the full joys of friendship. Others have their family; but to a solitary and an exile his friends are everything.

WILLA CATHER, *Shadow on the Rock*

Friendship is not possible between two women,
one of whom is very well dressed.

LAURIE COLWIN

Good books, like good friends, are few and chosen;
the more select, the more enjoyable.

LOUISA MAY ALCOTT

The easiest kind of relationship for me is with ten
thousand people. The hardest is with one.

JOAN BAEZ

Be generous and understanding. Let no one come to you
without feeling better and happier when they leave. Be the
living expression of God's kindness: with kindness on your
face…in your eyes…in your smile…in your warm greeting.

MOTHER TERESA

Writers seldom choose as friends those self-contained characters who are never in trouble, never unhappy or will never make mistakes, and always count their change when it is handed to them.

CATHERINE DRINKER BOWEN

Choose your friends carefully. Your enemies will choose you.

YASSIR ARAFAT

If I don't have friends, then I ain't nothing.

BILLIE HOLIDAY

The man who treasures his friends
is usually solid gold himself.

MARJORIE HOLMES

Friendship that flows from the heart cannot be frozen by adversity, as the water that flows from the spring cannot congeal in winter.

JAMES FENIMORE COOPER

Nobody sees a flower really; it is so small. We haven't time, and to see takes time—like to have a friend takes time.

GEORGIA O'KEEFFE

A friend i'the court is better than a penny in purse.

SHAKESPEARE, *Henry IV*

Friendship with oneself is all important, because without it one cannot be friends with anyone else in the world.

ELEANOR ROOSEVELT

Dear Diary:

Who says New York is an unfriendly place?

I went to a popular neighborhood diner for Sunday brunch. It was crowded. When I asked for a booth, I was told that singles were supposed to sit at small tables in the rear.

Two very attractive, well-dressed young men sitting nearby invited me to share their booth. "Why sit alone?" they asked.

I thought it over for one second and slid in alongside one of them. One was a playwright, the other a photographer. We talked about Broadway and Off Broadway theater, movies and restaurants. It was a lovely brunch, I hope as enjoyable for them as it was for me.

No, we didn't exchange business cards or phone numbers. After all, I'm 81 years old.

EVELYN MALINA, "METROPOLITAN DIARY,"
The New York Times

Acquaintance, n. A person whom we know well enough to borrow from, but not well enough to lend to.

AMBROSE BIERCE, *The Devil's Dictionary*

Friendship, n. A ship big enough to carry two in fair weather, but only one in foul.

AMBROSE BIERCE, *The Devil's Dictionary*

The making of friends, who are real friends,
is the best token we have of success in life.

EDWARD EVERETT HALE

Neither a borrower, nor a lender be;
for loan oft loses both itself and friend…

WILLIAM SHAKESPEARE, *Hamlet*

Why do people lament their follies for
which their friends adore them?

GERARD MANLEY HOPKINS

Every man can tell how many goats or sheep he possesses,
but not how many friends.

CICERO

Never contract friendship with
a man that is not better than thyself.

CONFUCIUS

. . . if I had to choose between betraying my country and
betraying my friend, I hope I should have the guts to betray
my country.

E. M. FORSTER

One friend in a lifetime is much;
two are many; three are hardly possible.

HENRY ADAMS

Never while I keep my senses shall
I compare anything to the delight of a friend.

HORACE

I'd like to be the sort of friend that you have been to me,
I'd like to be the help that you've been always glad to be;
I'd like to mean as much to you each minute of the day, as
you have meant old friend of mine, to me along the way.

EDGAR A. GUEST

Life is very short and there's no time
for fussing and fighting my friend.

JOHN LENNON/PAUL MCCARTNEY

Friendships are what our dreams are made of. We hold onto each other with its binding love. We stand close to each other, hand in hand, showing each other we understand. Some friends may come and go, but you are the truest friend I know.

ELSA MAXWELL

Remember, no man is a failure who has friends.

From *It's a Wonderful Life*

In New York City public school in 1922, I had a spelling teacher we named Maud the Mule. In order to teach us to spell "friend," she used to recite "A friend to the end!" over and over again.

SONIA, AGE 82

Close friends become family and family is the
true center of the universe.

DAVE MARINACCIO, *All I really need to
know I learned from watching Star Trek*

 True friends are those
seeking solitude together.

ABEL BONNARD

When the sun shines on you, you see your friends. Friends are
the thermometers by which one may judge the temperature of
our fortunes.

MARGUERITE BLESSINGTON

A true friend gives freely, advises justly, assists readily,
adventures boldly, takes all patiently, defends courageously,
and continues a friend unchangeable.

WILLIAM PENN

Your friends will know you better in the first minute you meet than your acquaintances will know you in a thousand years.

RICHARD BACH

And let your best be for your friend.
If he must know the ebb of your tide,
　　let him know its flood also.
For what is your friend that you should seek him
　　with hours to kill?
Seek him always with hours to live.
For it is his to fill your need, but not your emptiness.
And in the sweetness of friendship let there be laughter, and
　　sharing of pleasures.
For in the dew of little things the heart finds its morning
　　and is refreshed.

KAHLIL GIBRAN, *The Prophet*

It is more shameful to distrust our friends than to be deceived by them.

FRANCOIS DE LA ROCHEFOUCAULD.

Laughter is not at all a bad beginning for a friendship, and it is far the best ending for one.

OSCAR WILDE

A single rose can be my garden . . . a single friend, my world.

LEO BUSCAGLIA

"Oh, Diana, will you promise faithfully never to forget me, the friend of your youth, no matter what dearer friends may caress thee?"

"Indeed I will," sobbed Diana, "and I'll never have another bosom friend—I don't want to have. I couldn't love anybody as I love you—"

LUCY M. MONTGOMERY, *Anne of Green Gables*

A man's friendships are one of
the best measures of his worth.

CHARLES DARWIN

A man cannot be said to succeed
in this life who does not satisfy one friend.

HENRY DAVID THOREAU

The better part of one's life
consists of his friendships.

ABRAHAM LINCOLN

The holy passion of Friendship is so sweet and steady and
loyal and enduring a nature that it will last through a whole
lifetime, if not asked to lend money.

MARK TWAIN, *Pudd'nhead Wilson's Calendar*

Good company and good discourse
are the very sinews of virtue.

IZAAK WALTON, *The Compleat Angler*

I lay it down as a fact that if all men knew what others say of
them, there would not be four friends in the world.

BLAISE PASCAL, *Pensées*

I do then with my friends as I do with my books. I would
have them where I can find them, but I seldom use them.

RALPH WALDO EMERSON

And let there be no purpose in friendship
save the deepening of the spirit.

KAHLIL GIBRAN, *The Prophet*

He who has a thousand friends
Has not a friend to spare,
While he who has on enemy
Shall meet him everywhere.

RALPH WALDO EMERSON

So long as we are loved by others I should say that we are almost indispensable; and no man is useless while he has a friend.

ROBERT LOUIS STEVENSON

No guest is so welcome in a friend's house that he will not become a nuisance after three days.

TITUS MACCIUS PLAUTUS

A hedge between keeps friendship green.

PROVERB

Do not tell a friend anything you
would conceal from an enemy.

ARABIAN PROVERB

Don't allow the grass to grow on the path of friendship.

NATIVE AMERICAN PROVERB

With true friends . . . even water
drunk together is sweet enough.

CHINESE PROVERB

Santa Claus has the right idea: visit people once a year.

VICTOR BORGE

Friendship improves happiness, and abates misery, by doubling
our joys, and dividing our grief.

JOSEPH ADDISON, ENGLISH STATESMAN AND POET

Among true and real friends, all is common; and were ignorance and envy and superstition banished form the world, all mankind would be friends.

Percy Bysshe Shelley

When you choose your friends, don't be short-changed by choosing personality over character.

W. Somerset Maugham

Never explain—your friends do not need it and your enemies will not believe you anyway.

Elbert Hubbard, *The Roycroft*
Dictionary of a Book of Epigrams

I'm a controversial figure. My friends
either dislike me or hate me.

OSCAR LEVANT

I breathed a song into the air,
It fell to earth, I knew not where…
And the song, from beginning to end,
I found again in the heart of a friend.

HENRY WADSWORTH LONGFELLOW

A friend to all is a friend to none.

ARISTOTLE

A true friend is the greatest of all blessings, and the one that
we take the least care of all to acquire.

FRANCOIS DE LA ROCHEFOUCAULD

If I'm such a legend, then why am I so lonely?

JUDY GARLAND

The greatest sweetener of human life is friendship.

JOSEPH ADDISON

Treat your friends as you do your pictures,
and place them in their best light.

JENNIE CHURCHILL

Be slow to fall into friendship; but when thou art in, continue
firm and constant.

SOCRATES

To be emotionally committed to somebody is very difficult,
but to be alone is impossible.

STEPHEN SONDHEIM

A tree is known by its fruit; a man by his deeds. A good deed is never lost; he who sows courtesy reaps friendship, and he who plants kindness gathers love.

SAINT BASIL 329AD

The bird a nest, the spider a web, man friendship.

WILLIAM BLAKE

The one thing your friends will never forgive you is your happiness.

ALBERT CAMUS

You can make more friends in two weeks by becoming interested in other people than you can in two years by trying to get other people interested in you.

DALE CARNEGIE

Friendship is the shadow of evening,
it grows until the sun of life sets.

LaFontaine

No road is long with good company.

Turkish Proverb

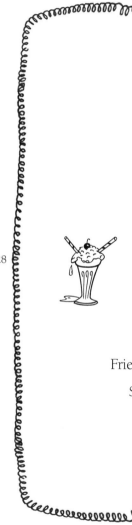

He hasn't an enemy in the
world. Only his friends hate him.

Gene Kelly about Frederic
March in *Inherit the Wind*

Friendship is like money, easier made than kept.

Samuel Butler, English poet 1612-1680

Friendship is like a sheltering tree.

Samuel Coleridge

Be courteous to all, but intimate with few, and let those few be well tried before you give them your confidence. True friendship is a plant of slow growth and must undergo and withstand the shocks of adversity before it is entitled to the appellation.

GEORGE WASHINGTON

Friends do not live in harmony mere,
as some say, but in melody.

HENRY DAVID THOREAU

My father always used to say that when you die, if you've got five real friends, then you've had a great life.

LEE IACOCCA

A friend is one who knows you and loves you just the same.

ELBERT HUBBARD, *The Roycroft Dictionary of a Book of Epigrams*

You're my friend—
What a thing friendship is,
world without end!
How it gives the heart and soul a stir-up!

ROBERT BROWNING

Friendship is the hardest thing in the world to explain. It's not something you learn in school. But if you haven't learned the meaning of friendship, you really haven't learned anything.

MUHAMMAD ALI

A true friend is the best possession.

BENJAMIN FRANKLIN

I decided to stop drinking with creeps.
I decided to drink only with friends.
I've lost 30 pounds.

ERNEST HEMINGWAY

The best time to make friends is before you need them.

ETHEL BARRYMORE

A friend knows how to allow for mere quantity
your talk, and only replies to the quality.

WILLIAM DEAN HOWELLS

Life is a chronicle of friendship. Friends create the world
anew each day. Without their loving care, courage would not
suffice to keep hearts strong for life.

HELEN KELLER

Fame is the scentless sunflower, with gaudy crown of gold;
But friendship is the breathing rose, with sweets in every fold.

OLIVER WENDELL HOLMES, "No Time Like the Old Time"

To Lead a Good Life: When somebody's nice to you, don't take advantage of it. You don't ride a free horse to death.

Sadie and Bessie Delaney,
Delaney Sisters' Book of Everyday Wisdom

True friendship is like sound health—the value of it is seldom known until it is lost.

Charles Caleb Colton, english author and clergyman

Whenever a friend succeeds, a little something in me dies.

Gore Vidal

When one it trying to do something beyond one's known powers it is useless to seek the approval of friends. Friends are at their best in moments of defeat.

Henry Miller

Friends are thieves of time.

FRANCIS BACON

A real friend walks in when
the rest of the world walks out.

WALTER WINCHELL

I never considered a difference of opinion in politics, in religion,
in philosophy, as cause for withdrawing from a friend.

THOMAS JEFFERSON

Think where man's glory most begins and ends
And say my glory was I had such friends.

WILLIAM BUTLER YEATS

Just thinking about a friend makes you want to do a happy dance, because a friend is someone who loves you in spite of your faults.

CHARLES M. SCHULZ

I choose my friends for their good looks, my acquaintances for their characters, and my enemies for their brains.

OSCAR WILDE, The Picture of Dorian Gray

To hear complaints with patience,
even when complaints are vain, is
one of the duties of friendship.

DR. SAMUEL JOHNSON

Friendship is not necessary, like philosophy, like art . . . It has no survival value; rather it is one of those things that give value to survival.

C. S. LEWIS, author of The Chronicles of Narnia

No one is completely unhappy
at the failure of his best friend.

GROUCHO MARX

Men kick friendship around like a football, but it doesn't
seem to crack. Women treat it like glass and it goes to pieces.

ANNE MORROW LINDBERGH

I desire so to conduct the affairs of this administration that if
at the end, when I come to lay down the reigns of power,
I have lost every other friend on earth, I shall at least have
one friend left, and that friend shall be down inside of me.

ABRAHAM LINCOLN

Of all the gifts that a wise providence
grants us to make life full and happy,
friendship is the most beautiful.

EPICURUS

When true friends meet in adverse hour;
'Tis like a sunbeam through a shower.

SIR WALTER SCOTT

True happiness
Consists not in the multitude of friends,
But in the worth and choice.

BEN JONSON

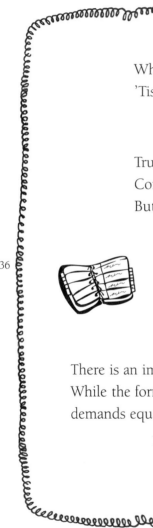

Laughter is the shortest
distance between two people.

VICTOR BORGE

There is an important difference between love and friendship.
While the former delights in extremes and opposites, the latter
demands equality.

MADAME DE MAINTENON, consort of
King Louis XIV

The friend who holds your hand and says the wrong thing is made of dearer stuff than the one who stays away.

BARBARA KINGSOLVER

No man can be happy without a friend, nor be sure of his friend till he is unhappy.

THOMAS FULLER

It is not a lack of love, but a lack of friendship that makes unhappy marriages.

FRIEDRICH NIETZSCHE

Though friendship is not quick to burn, it is explosive stuff.

MAY SARTON

A doubtful friend is worse than a certain enemy. Let a man be one thing or the other, and we then know how to meet him.

AESOP

Depth of friendship does not
depend on length of acquaintance.

SIR RABINDRANATH TAGORE, Bengali writer

I want someone to laugh with me, someone to be grave with me, someone to please me and help my discrimination with his or her own remarks, and at times, no doubt, to admire my acuteness and penetration.

ROBERT BURNS

The worst solitude is to be
destitute of sincere friendship.

FRANCIS BACON

Love is only chatter,
Friends are all that matter.

FRANK GELETT BURGESS,
American humorist

But of all plagues, good Heaven, thy wrath can send,
Save, save, oh save me from the candid friend!

GEORGE CANNING, British statesman

Wishing to be friends is quick work,
but friendship is slow-ripening fruit.

ARISTOTLE

Histories are more full of examples
of the fidelity of dogs than of friends.

ALEXANDER POPE

He who throws away a friend is as
bad as he who throws away his life.

SOPHOCLES

He makes no friend who never made a foe.

ALFRED, LORD TENNYSON

Friendship is the gift of the gods,
and the most precious boon to man.

BENJAMIN DISRAELI

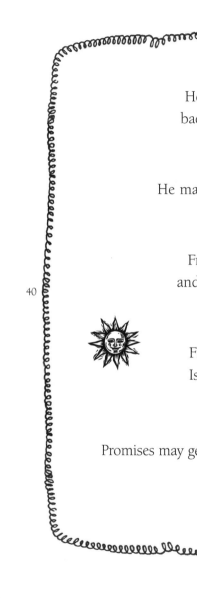

Friendship, of itself a holy tie,
Is made more sacred by adversity.

JOHN DRYDEN

Promises may get friends but it's performance that keeps them.

BENJAMIN FRANKLIN

Blessed are they who have the gift of making friends, for it is one of God's best gifts. It involves many things, but above all, the power of going out of one's self, and appreciating whatever is noble and loving in another.

THOMAS HUGHES

Greater love hath no man than this,
that a man lay down his life for his friends.

JOHN 14:13, NEW TESTAMENT

Friendship is the marriage of the soul;
and this marriage is subject to divorce.

VOLTAIRE

Sometimes you have to get to know someone really well to realize you're really strangers.

MARY TYLER MOORE

Four be the things I am wiser to know:
Idleness, sorrow, a friend, and a foe.

DOROTHY PARKER

It is the friends you can call up at 4 A.M. that matter.

MARLENE DIETRICH

It is wise to apply the refined oil of
politeness to the mechanism of friendship.

COLETTE

Next to having a staunch friend is the
pleasure of having a brilliant enemy.

OSCAR WILDE

Of all my imaginary friends, I don't think there
was one that I didn't end up having to kill.

JACK HANDY, *Fuzzy Memories*

True friendship is never serene.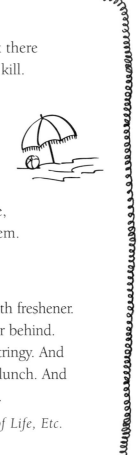

MARIE DE SÉVIGNÉ

I do not want people to be agreeable,
as it saves me that trouble of liking them.

JANE AUSTEN

A friend is someone who tells you you need a breath freshener.
And that your skirt makes funny bulges across your behind.
And that the veal in your veal Marsala is dry and stringy. And
that Marjorie Cooper is meeting your husband for lunch. And
I think I need something friendlier than friendship.

JUDITH VIORST, *Love, Guilt & The Meaning of Life, Etc.*

Ferengi Rule of Acquisition: Never place friendship above profit.

Star Trek: Deep Space Nine

I know that we're good enough friends that I could just call you on the phone, but I thought that a letter would be preferable for two reasons. One, often it's easier to say things in a letter than it is to say them in person. And two, you don't seem to be answering my phone calls anymore.

ELLEN DEGENERES, *My Point . . . and I do have one*

One should only have acquaintances
and never make friends.

W. SOMERSET MAUGHAM

May God defend me from my friends:
I can defend myself from my enemies.

VOLTAIRE

Nothing so fortifies a friendship as a belief on the part of one friend that he is superior to the other.

HONORE DE BALZAC

We're not an old married couple who can't live together and can't live apart; we're two men who've been friends for 30 years. Occasionally you want to strangle even the closest of friends.

MICK JAGGER about KEITH RICHARDS

Don't walk in front of me, I may not follow.
Don't walk behind me, I may not lead.
Walk beside me and be my friend.

ALBERT CAMUS

In the world of relationships, probably the most complicated, uncommon, hard to find hard to keep, and most rewarding has got to be friendship.

LAUREN BACALL, *Now*

Girls at the mall are not just shopping. Women chatting over coffee are not just sharing news. Instead, they are involved in intricate patternings of love and conflict that inexorably shape and change who they are.

TERRI APTER, PH.D. and
RUTHELLEN JOSSELSON, PH.D., *Best Friends*

If you think you have given enough, think again.
There is always more to give and someone to give it to.

NORMAN VINCENT PEALE

Adversity not only draws people together, but brings forth that beautiful inward friendship, just as the cold winter forms ice figures on window panes, which the warmth of the sun effaces.

KIERKEGAARD

There is more hunger for love and
appreciation in this world than for bread.

MOTHER TERESA

A little selective suppression, even when we're certain we're
right, does more than win friends and influence people. It
enhances feelings of respect and love and is the stuff of which
lasting relationships are made.

LEO BUSCAGLIA, *Born for Love*

Just as the wave cannot exist for itself, but must always
participate in the swell of the ocean, so we can never
experience life by ourselves, but must always share the
experience of life that takes place all around us.

ALBERT SCHWEITZER

People change and forget to tell each other.

LILLIAN HELLMAN

Sign in a Third Avenue
Diner in New York City:

Friendship is our motto
courtesy is our business
Whatever you ask
is never a task.

We cannot live only for ourselves. A thousand fibers connect us
with our fellow men; and along these fibers, as sympathetic
threads, our actions run as causes, and they come back as effects.

HERMAN MELVILLE

I will pay attention to the people I have gathered in my life and
ask myself what I have to give to them and they to me. There is
that old saying, "Show me your friends and I will show you who
you are"—it is truer than we realize. My friends are my mirror,
showing me the way to become the best person I can be.

SUZANNE SOMERS, *365 Ways to Change Your Life*

Keep your friends close, but your enemies closer.

MARIO PUZO, *The Godfather*

Our most intimate friend is not he to whom
we show the worst, but the best, of our nature.

NATHANIEL HAWTHORNE

May God preserve me from the love
of a friend who will never dare to rebuke me.

THOMAS MERTON, *No Man Is an Island*

The only way to have a friend is to be one.

RALPH WALDO EMERSON

49

When they are alone they want to be with others, and when they are with others they want to be alone. After all, human beings are like that.

GERTRUDE STEIN

The richer your friends, the more they will cost you.

ELISABETH MARBURY, Literary Agent

You can choose your friends,
but you only have one mother.

MAX SHULMAN

Gayle [King Bumpus] helps keep me grounded and centered. She adds balance to my life. We've been friends since 1976 and have a relationship like none other. We're like blood sisters.

OPRAH WINFREY, The Uncommon
Wisdom of Oprah Winfrey

LOVE AND FRIENDSHIP

Love is like the wild rose-briar,
Friendship is like the holly-tree—
The holly is dark when the rose-briar blooms
But which will bloom most constantly?

EMILY BRONTE

The telephone is a good way to talk
to people without having to offer them a drink.

FRAN LEBOWITZ

Good communication is just as stimulating as black coffee,
and just as hard to sleep after.

ANNE MORROW LINDBERGH

Don't accept your dog's admiration as
conclusive evidence that you are wonderful.

ANN LANDERS

If you're ever in a jam,
Here I am.
If you're ever in a mess
SOS
If you ever feel so happy you land in jail
I'm your bail.
It's friendship
Friendship
Just a perfect blendship
When other friendships have been forgot
Ours
Will still be hot.

COLE PORTER, "Friendship"

He makes no friend who never made a foe.

TENNYSON

52

. . . a friend doesn't go on a diet when you are fat. A friend never defends a husband who gets his wife an electric skillet for her birthday by saying, "At least, he's not one to carouse around at night."

A friend will tell you she saw your old boyfriend—and he's a priest.

A friend will babysit your children when they are contagious.

A friend when asked what you think of a home permanent will lie. A friend will threaten to kill anyone who tries to come into the fitting room when you are trying on bathing suits. But most of all, a friend will not make each minute of every day count and screw it up for the rest of us.

ERMA BOMBECK, *The Grass is Always
Greener over the Septic Tank*

The average dog is a nicer person than the average person.

ANDREW A. ROONEY

When I was a kid, I had two friends, and they were imaginary and they would only play with each other.

RITA RUDNER

The statistics on sanity are that one out of every four Americans is suffering from some form of mental illness. Think of your three best friends. If they are okay, then it's you.

RITA MAE BROWN

It is not good to be alone, even in Paradise.

YIDDISH PROVERB

Do not protect yourself by a fence,
but rather by your friends.

CZECH PROVERB

Who seeks a faultless friend remains friendless.

Turkish proverb

Friends are like fiddle-strings, they must not be screwed too tight.

H. G. Bohn, *A Hand-Book of Proverbs* (1855)

As children, almost all of us had an imaginary friend of one kind or another. Our parents took these friends seriously—inquiring about their health, maybe even setting a place at dinner for them—because our society encourages and embraces the imagination of a child. As we grow older, however, reality is supposed to set in.

Bob Weinstein, co-chairman of Miramax Films in *New York Times Magazine*

Choose thy friends like thy books, few but choice.

JAMES HOWELL, *PROVERBS*, 1659

If you have one true friend, you have more than your share.

THOMAS FULLER, *Gnomologia*, 1732

I argue very well. Ask any of my remaining friends.

DAVE BARRY

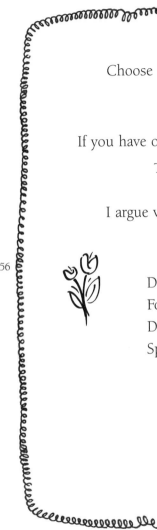

Do not save your loving speeches
For your friends till they are dead;
Do not write them on their tombstones,
Speak them rather now instead.

ANNA CUMMINS

Money can't buy friends, but you
can get a better class of enemy.

SPIKE MILLIGAN

56

In this world you will have to make your own way.
To do that you must have friends.
You can make friends by being honest and you can keep them
by being steadfast.
You must keep in mind that friends worth having will in the
long run expected as much from you as they give to you.

Elizabeth Hutchinson Jackson to her
14-year-old son, Andrew Jackson

If you make one new friend a day, at the end of the year
you'll be stuck with 365 new friends.

Milton Berle, *More of the Best of Milton
Berle's Private Joke File*

We read that we ought to forgive our enemies; but we do not
read that we ought to forgive our friends.

Cosimo de Medici

Alone, all alone
Nobody, but nobody
Can make it out here alone.

MAYA ANGELOU

When a friend calls to me from the road
And slows his horse to a meaning walk,
I don't stand still and look around
On all the hills I haven't hoed,
And shout from where I am, What is it?
No, not as there is a time to talk.
I thrust my hoe in the mellow ground,
Blade-end up and five feet tall,
And plod: I go up to the stone wall
For a friendly visit.

ROBERT FROST

It seems to me that trying to live without friends is like milking a bear to get cream for your morning coffee. It is a whole lot of trouble, and then not worth much after you get it.

Zora Neale Hurston

Yes'm, old friends is always best, 'less you can catch a new one that's fit to make an old one out of.

Sarah Orne Jewett

Each friend represents a world in us, a world possibly not born until they arrive, and it is only by this meeting that a new world is born.

Anaïs Nin

The loneliest woman in the world is a woman without a close woman friend.

GEORGE SANTAYANA, *The Life of Reason*

I've discovered a way to stay friends forever—
There's really nothing to it.
I simply tell you what to do
And you do it!

SHEL SILVERSTEIN, "Friendship"

We are all travelers in the wilderness of this world, and the best we can find in our travels is an honest friend.

ROBERT LOUIS STEVENSON

No person is your friend who demands
your silence, or denies your right to grow.

ALICE WALKER

Friendship demands attention.

THOMAS MOORE, IRISH POET

To cement a new friendship, especially between foreigners or
persons of a different social world, a spark with which both
were secretly charged must fly from person to person, and cut
across the accidents of place and time.

CORNELIA OTIS SKINNER, *The Ape in Me*

Then there are friends like Kirk and Spock. Yin and yang, the opposite sides of the same circle, perfect complements to each other. Kirk needs Spock's coolness and calculation. Spock needs Kirk's gut instincts and aggressiveness. They complete each other.

DAVE MARINACCIO, *All I really need to know
I learned from watching Star Trek*

The love of our neighbor in all its fullness simply means being able to say, "What are you going through?"

SIMONE WEIL

True friends stab you in the front.

OSCAR WILDE

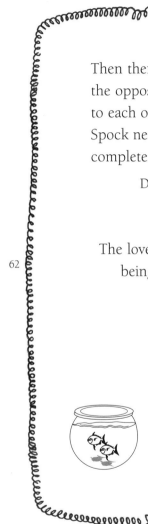

A brother may not be a friend,
but a friend is always a brother.

BENJAMIN FRANKLIN

"You have been my friend. That in itself is a tremendous thing. I wove my webs for you because I liked you. After all, what's a life, anyway? We're born, we live a little while, we die. A spider's life can't help being something of a mess, with all this trapping and eating flies. By helping you, perhaps I was trying to lift up my life a trifle. Heaven knows anyone's life can stand a little of that."

CHARLOTTE, in *Charlotte's Web* by E. B. White

Friends are generally of the same sex, for when men and women agree, it is only in the conclusions; their reasons are always different.

GEORGE SANTAYANA, *Persons and Places: The Middle Span*

I'm a controversial figure. My friends either dislike me or hate me.

TONI MORRISON, speech, Sarah Lawrence
College, Bronxville, New York, 1978

I no doubt deserved my enemies, but
I don't believe I deserved my friends.

WALT WHITMAN

A friend is a present you give yourself.

ROBERT LOUIS STEVENSON

The wing of friendship never moults a feather.

CHARLES DICKENS